PEARLS UNDER THE LAMPSTAND

Pearls
Under the
Lampstand

By T.D. Page

Pearls Under the Lampstand by T.D. Page

Copyright ©2025 T.D. Page

Cover art created with Microsoft AI assistance

Cover Formatted by Essqué Productions

Published by KDP Independent Publishing Platform
May 2025

ISBN: 9798281010771

DEDICATION

Grandma,
Thank you for who you are and for Who you love.

May your legacy continue to grow and be a
blessing to all.

ACKNOWLEDGMENTS

I'm grateful to God first and foremost for the gift of writing and being able to share my thoughts with you, the reader.

I'm grateful for the encouragement of my family and friends through the years.

Thank you to the many who have helped me put "Pearls Under the Lampstand" together.

A special thanks to my sister for helping me find the perfect title.

Thank you Bridget, Jo, Lorraine, MJ, Rose, Sara, Stephen and my fellow prayer warriors for your prayers, extra input, and advice.

PEARLS UNDER THE LAMPSTAND

Contents

One:
Tapestries

When I was young, my aunt taught me how to embroider and cross-stitch. During one of the lessons, she mentioned how our lives are a lot like tapestries. We see the underside, on which the threads run in chaotic directions and are tied off in random spots to secure them in place when we change colors or end a line of stitches. She said God sees the topside, where the beautiful picture is shown. He knows where each thread must be directed to make the tapestry perfect.

As I grew up, I heard different versions of the illustration. But the story always told how we see the bottom of the tapestry and God sees the top, so we should trust Him in the middle of the hard knots of life.

However, I recently had the chance to think on tapestries differently. Sometimes we are the ones on the completed side, seeing the beauty, while God is behind the scenes, fixing spots underneath we may not even be aware of.

For example, one Sunday, I dressed in my favorite slacks. While deciding what to wear with them, I wavered between putting on a tank top with a shirt over it or just a nice blouse. Looking at the blouse, I kept wondering what would happen if I got too hot or needed to take off my over shirt. Puzzling over why I would need to do that, I still chose the dual layers for comfort. I walked out of the house feeling fabulous and ready for the day.

At church, my body indicated the need for the facilities. While there, I happened to glance down. Boldly staring right back at me was a big split in the seam of my pants. I realized I definitely needed my over shirt, and I was grateful I had chosen to listen to that Still, Small Voice.

Another flip-flopping of my tapestry of life happened in the same month, but it was much more drastic in its possible outcomes.

I can usually hear when the brakes on my car begin the high-pitched whine that lets me know they may need changed before their maintenance date. But the weather had been very cold, which meant I had the heater going. The sound of the blower drowned out most other noises.

After a couple of weeks had passed, the weather turned warmer. I rolled my windows down to enjoy the fresh spring air, stepped on the brakes, and heard the telltale screech. I mentioned it to my husband and didn't think a lot about it.

Over the next week or so, instead of the occasional squeal, my brakes started making a loud grinding noise. I told my husband the sounds were getting worse, and he promised to have a look over the weekend.

That Friday, a dear friend of mine went into the hospital. I decided to visit her the next morning. As everyone knows, having a house with children, dogs, a cat, and the general chaos of life can change plans rapidly. That day was no exception. Finally, by mid-afternoon, I was ready to go with my husband to visit my friend at the hospital.

2

We pulled out of the driveway, and he said, "I want to ask our neighbor to look at the brakes first."

We drove to the neighbor's house, wincing each time we had to stop. Our neighbor took our car for a trip around the block and delivered the bad news: The front brakes were completely gone, and the back ones were halfway there.

Wait!

What?

How had I missed the signs?

I had been driving my kids to school, going to church, and taking them to youth group across town… with no brakes!

Needless to say, my husband and I "grounded' the vehicle and started figuring out what we were going to do.

My mom had just picked up her second car from the mechanic, who had performed general maintenance on it. She said we could use it until ours was repaired. Having a great mom who shares her vehicle is beyond getting spoiled, but here's the catch. My dad was out of town and should have gotten back that week. He'd been delayed getting home due to unforeseen circumstances, which left the secondary car available.

While I was enjoying the bliss of spring weather, God was being the brakes for my family. When I get to heaven and see my whole tapestry of life, I'm pretty sure that particular moment will have a huge knot on the underside with a lot of threads holding it together.

Two:
Jennifer's Sunshine

I walked into the room one day

And you were there, full of sunshine.

Your smile lit the place up,

Your laughter was like multiple bells ringing.

MS didn't scare you.

You were tough.

MS didn't steal your joy.

You were too ornery.

Every day we talked, our friendship grew

And every day we talked, I walked away refreshed by your sunshine.

I found out that your sunshine has suddenly been darkened by clouds,

And my tears became their rain in that loss.

Yet through it all,

The memory of your sunshine

Still beams through the water flowing,

Creating rainbows,

Bittersweet colors that taunt and cheer simultaneously.

Last week your sunshine left the Earth, but your rainbows remain.

Three:
Tomayto, Tomahto, Part One

In the summer of 2020, my family planted some tomatoes in the front yard. We like to make our own sauce, eat them directly, and eventually can them for stew in the winter if we get enough.

The five plants grew to about waist high and bushy, rather big for a semi-arid climate. Most of July and all of August, we enjoyed the different varieties: yellow pear, Roma, Cherry, and a medium sized one I don't remember the name of. Near the end of August, our area received news that a major cold front was coming in with sleet and snow.

In my younger years, my mom had taught me how to bag a plant to keep the warmer air trapped around it and therefore prevent damage from freezing. We decided to pull off as many tomatoes as we could find, green or ripe, and bag the plants in hopes they could last a bit longer.

I brought out a large box, about three feet wide and as high as my knee. My husband, four kids, and I started gleaning from the plants. When each of us finished a plant, the next person in line would go over the same one to make sure nothing was missed. Every single time, a branch would be lifted or turned and there would be clusters of tomatoes peeking at us. We filled the box, grabbed another one about half its size, and filled it as well.

By this time, even though the plants were still full of tomatoes, we called it quits because the storm was almost upon us.

I sent the kids to the car because we were visiting my mother that evening, and my husband loaded the two boxes into the back.

I grabbed some heavy-duty backyard trash bags and started bagging the tomato plants inside them. Because the plants were clustered tightly in a row, I had to cut the bags and tape them together to form a tent. My husband came to help me, and by the time we were done, sleet was already coming down hard and covering the grass.

We prayed a quick prayer over the tomato plants and jumped into the car. Everyone paused their chatter for a moment before talking and laughing excitedly over one another.

"Did you see how many tomatoes we got?"

"I kept moving a branch I'd just cleaned off, and more would be on the other side!"

"There weren't that many tomatoes to start with; now there are even more on the plants!"

"Tomatoes multiplied right before my very eyes!"

"We're going to have a feast tonight and when the others ripen up!"

A pause. Then:

"Thank You Jesus for our tomatoes and showing us this miracle!"

Four:
Is Your Postage Paid?

When I was little, I learned a lot by observing the world around me and then putting those things into practice as best I could. When I was six or seven years old, sticker collecting was very popular.

I had a Pepto Bismol-pink sticker album where I kept my prized treasures. It had a plastic insert with six pockets to store extras for trading. That was followed by sturdy paper pages with themes such as "puffy stickers", "smelly stickers", "shiny stickers", etc. to place my keepers. I was always on the lookout for new types to add or trade, and that album went with me almost everywhere.

One sunny summer afternoon, my mom asked me to check the mailbox. As I was walking back up the driveway with the mail, I noticed a peculiar-looking sticker on the corner of the front envelope. In fact, all of the envelopes had one.

"Mom, why are these stickers on all the envelopes?" I placed the mail on the counter and pointed at each upper right corner.

She glanced over. "Those aren't stickers, they're stamps. You put one on the envelope so the mailman can bring it to the person you write to."

The wheels in my head began to turn as I thought about a letter I'd been getting ready to send.

"Mom, can I have this envelope, please?" I grabbed a newly emptied one.

"Yeah, that's fine."

I clutched the empty envelope in my hand and ran upstairs, calculating where the mailman would be and if I could catch him fast enough. It was worth a try.

I found my scissors and carefully cut the stamp off the old envelope. Next, I pasted it onto my new one, put the letter in, sealed and addressed it, and went back to my mom.

"Mom, can I go catch the mailman so I can send this letter?'

She looked up from her cooking. "Only go as far as the next street up. Otherwise you'll have to wait until tomorrow."

Barely waiting to hear the last of her answer, I tore out the door and up the hilly sidewalk to the next street. Yes! The postal truck was halfway down the block.

I caught up to the mailman and held out the letter as I tried to catch my breath.

The man looked at it and then at me. "I can't mail that." His voice was kind but firm.

I was confused. "But it has a stamp. Right there."

He shook his head. "No, it needs a new stamp. That one's been used." He pointed to some ink lines across it.

"But my mom said I just needed one to send a letter." I wasn't trying to complain but my voice betrayed some of my frustration.

Again he shook his head. "She meant a new one. These letters cost money to send. When we mail the letter, we add an ink line to the stamp to show it's been used. Each time, you'll need to buy another stamp, or you'd be mailing your letter for free."

I nodded my understanding, greatly disappointed. I made my way slowly back home to reflect on what I'd learned.

Now, years later, I can laugh at my misunderstanding, and appreciate that I can send a letter across the country for less than a dollar. However, I also realize that God shows us life lessons in everything, including my mix up with postage.

For example, there are many thoughts that say all paths eventually lead to God or paradise, but Jesus says that He is the Way, the Truth, and the Light. No one goes to the Father except through Him.

We learn in Ephesians 1:13-14 from Paul that when we hear the word of truth, the gospel of our salvation, and believe in Him, we are sealed with the Holy Spirit, who is the guarantee of our inheritance until we acquire possession of it, to the praise of His glory. Paul also tells us in 2 Corinthians 4:14 that "knowing He who raised the Lord Jesus will raise us also with Jesus and bring us with you into His presence."

Jesus is like our envelope. He covers us with His blood, and He paid the price for our way. When we accept and believe in Him and His salvation, He gives us our "stamp", the Holy Spirit, to show that we're paid for.

So my question is this: Is your postage to God paid for?

Five:
Mrs. Banks' Voicemail

Most of the time when we think of godly people, a pious and formal image of a priest or saint comes to mind. Mrs. Banks definitely didn't fit that image, though she was quite godly.

We met Mrs. Banks when she came as the weekly in-home nurse assigned to care for my son's various IV lines while he waited for a new heart. She was a beautiful lady inside and out. She gave off a welcoming and relaxed presence that could calm a room and a patient like I'd not seen before. She was the one my son would greet warmly and cooperate with to get things done.

As the months passed, Mrs. Banks and I got to know each other pretty well, and I found out she was an author, too. For Christmas that year, she gifted me her book, *Wrong Feet First: A Gift of Stories for Your Inside-Out Kind of Day*, which was her autobiography. My respect for her had always been high, but after reading about her journey, it shot through the roof.

A few years ago, she asked her friends on social media what would be a good gift for her child to bring to his host family as a foreign exchange student. We all offered her many ideas, and she was so excited for him. About halfway through his trip, we received a message through her page from him. Mrs. Banks had suddenly passed away overnight.

I was in shock. This vibrant lady who had blessed so many families was gone in an instant. I cherished the memories of her as I mourned her loss and prayed for her kids.

About six months later, I was cleaning up my voicemail box and discovered a special treasure: I still had a voicemail from Mrs. Banks! Her voice filled my ears as tears flooded my eyes. A piece of her life remained to remind me of her unconditional love for my son and my family.

I have that voicemail to listen to today, but the true gift from Mrs. Banks is the Still, Small voice behind hers. It reminds me of God's love as well, surpassing time and sending encouragement.

Six:
Pumpkins, Pumpkins!

A few years ago, my family moved across the country. That in itself is a huge task, but it also meant changes in climate and altitude, which bring their own learning curves. For example, I figured out after about two weeks that I needed to cook my foods at a much lower temperature or I'd burn the snot out of them.

It also might seem rather obvious, coming from a semi-arid desert to a humid, warmer South, but another difference was the vegetation.

I'd been forewarned by a dear friend of mine who'd lived here previously. With a big smile on her face, she said, "You put a seed in the ground, and it grows."

"Okay," I laughed in reply. "I would hope so!"

She shook her head. "No, you don't understand, my friend. You put a seed in the ground, and it GROWS! It's a miracle!"

Looking back, I remember thinking I was finally going to have a chance at a successful garden. Little did I know what my friend was telling me until a couple years later.

Up to that point I'd just assumed my large tomato plants were due to their variety, as they were anywhere from two to four feet tall. As they began to grow the second year, our neighbors whom we share the property with noticed a squash plant also growing.

I'd tried unsuccessfully growing a zucchini plant the

previous year, so we thought maybe it was a late bloomer and put a support cage around it to help keep the vines off the ground.

It kept growing. And spreading out.

And growing. And getting longer.

After about a month, we realized it was in fact a pumpkin plant. But by then it was too late to transplant it without the risk of killing it. I wasn't worried though because in the year prior, our pumpkin plant by the shed hadn't gone too crazy. Trying to figure out how it got there, I remembered our heirloom pumpkin that had started to decompose on our porch in the early spring before I could make pumpkin pie from it.

As the months went by, I was astounded at the enormity of this plant. It began to take over my front lawn, putting down tendrils and growing new branches. The leaves were as big as my medium-sized dog's head. By July, we were seeing pumpkins. Every day seemed to bring more blossoms, and every week the pumpkins continued to grow. By September, we had at least ten full sized pumpkins and even more baby ones.

In mid-September, we began harvesting the ones turning more orange. We gave some to friends who wanted them and lined the rest up on the porch to cure for the winter.

The plant continued to grow. The vines were now climbing up and through the bushes by our front window. I had to divert the ground ones trying to cross our driveway. They began to stretch around the corner of the house. I told my neighbor I now understood how Cinderella could have a carriage from one of these things.

When all was said and done, we got over 20 pumpkins from

this one plant, fifteen of which we kept. I began to feel like Laura Ingalls Wilder's Ma as I processed pumpkin after pumpkin. It was worth it when we had our pies at Thanksgiving. So delicious! When December came around, my time to process the pumpkins became constrained. So I let the last five stay on the porch until I could get to them. I managed to take care of two of them before the huge frost in January.

I felt guilty for not processing the final three pumpkins, but I knew that God would help me use them in some fashion. I took one to the back yard and chopped it up for my chickens, who absolutely loved their treat. I also discovered inside the shell and pulp were sprouted seedlings, ready to grow for the next season. The other two had them as well. I collected the baby plants and planted them in a starter box.

Note: Don't put a starter box on a brick wall in the sun. I accidentally cooked those poor seedlings. It was very disappointing. Remember the chicken treat, though? God still used these to plant some "bonus blessings,' as a friend of mine calls them, and we are looking forward to the next harvest season.

God also reminded me that His plans and timing are perfect. He gives us what we need when we need it. In the fall it was pumpkin puree. For this new year, seedlings to bless others and continue the harvest seasons. And in between, feeding our animals.

Overall, I learned my lesson. When a seed gets planted in the ground here, it will GROW.

Seven:
Nothing Wasted

For as long as I can remember, I've loved to read. When I had a book, especially a story of some type, I'd focus on it until it was done – almost excluding anything else. I even had a method of keeping distractions away by going to my room or a quiet corner and piling as many fluffy pillows around and behind me as I could.

One day my dad came to me with a small book in his hand. "Good morning." He held out the book. It had a black and white picture of a young, smiling girl with the title *Alex: the Life of a Child*. "I thought you might be interested in this book. The girl is close to your age."

I practically snatched the book from his hands while trying to be polite in my acceptance of it. "Thank you, dad!"

I ran to my room and landed on my pillow pile, ready to learn about this girl named Alex.

It turned out the book was a biography and autobiography of Alex and her father. Alex had been born with cystic fibrosis, which caused her to have multiple health problems in her short life. What stood out to me in the midst of her trials was how her family chose to live and enjoy every moment to the fullest, despite the diagnosis.

When my fourth child was born, he too had a life-threatening illness: Hypoplastic Left Heart Syndrome (HLHS). What that meant was he literally had half of a developed heart. Through multiple surgeries and many answered prayers, plus eventually a hearttransplant, my son has been strong and healthy.

While my son was still young, I remembered the book about Alex. The memory prompted me to ask my dad why he'd given the book to me at such a young age because the story had truly shaped how my family handled my own son's struggles by celebrating every moment of life to the fullest.

My dad simply answered, "I'm not sure. It just seemed right at the time."

This is one example in many of how God has placed an event or person in my life that would either help me or prepare me to help others. I look forward to the day when I view my life with Christ and get to see how He used all the events, big and small, for His glory.

.

Eight:
A Tale of Three Hearts

A mother's love encompassed her child's heart, wanting to make it whole.

Trusting in the Savior's love.

Understanding, and yet still learning, how to cherish every moment and day, not knowing if it would be the last.

Tears.

Laughter.

More tears.

More laughter.

And repeat...

And then, the call.

It was unexpected.

It was not forgotten, but also not the first thought.

Or the second.

Or the 20th.

The Call.

A new heart. Her child would either keep going, or be with the Savior.

Praying for yet another miracle.

Trying to trust.

Trusting.

Trying to trust again.

Seeing other friends and their children...

Waiting...

So much waiting...

His new heart beat again.

The gift from another family's loss... becoming a gift of life for hers.

Always. ALWAYS. Cherishing...

Each...

And...

Every...

Day.

A tale of four hearts:

The Savior's, the mother's, the child's *old* one becoming *new*.

Nine:
The Best Hope

What is hope? According to dictionary.com, hope is defined as the following: "noun: the feeling that what is wanted can be had or that events will turn out for the best."

Recently, a country I've visited multiple times and grown to love started to lose hope. There were many facets and different groups involved in the response to the situation; most in a negative way. Neighbors were turning against neighbors, businesses were being vandalized and destroyed, land was getting taken over, and people's lives were being threatened more and more.

The country was becoming divided, and any hope of reuniting it into a strong nation was quickly falling away. As I read new reports, or heard from friends, my heart broke for the people. I wanted to rush over and do what I could to help solve the problem. But there was a flaw to my plan. How could an issue of such magnitude be changed overnight? How could ugliness be unraveled and recreated into a beautiful tapestry?

The beginning of an answer came in the form of Rugby. One of the national teams had been struggling, so a new coach was brought in. Through hard work and effort, the new coach not only took the team to the finals, but also to a world championship.

How did rugby bring hope to the country? People from all backgrounds came together to cheer on their team. They stood side by side in a crowded airport to greet the team returning

19

triumphantly after the championship. For a moment, there was peace. The rugby team briefly showed the country how to unite over a common cause.

There is now hope again for the country. There is hope that one day the nation will build equality among all people, and that wounds among the divided cultures might be healed.

The fragile hope built by a rugby team may last a few months or a few years, but it will eventually fade away. The question that remains is, how can any of us have an eternal hope?

I have found in my own life that the answer lies in Psalm 39:7, "But now Lord, what do I look for? My hope is in You."

Many times in my own life, hope would start to run out. Each and every time, the loss of hope would be stopped through Jesus Christ. My circumstances didn't always change, but I knew I could hope for good to come from them. I have my own Champion who knows when I need the extra boost of hope through a victory in life. He is a Champion for anyone who asks Him to be.

What kind of hope do you have today?

Ten:
Abba, Daddy

As my family was on the way to church one sunny morning, I happened to glance down at my hair in its braid. I noticed the way it changed from brown to blonde with copper red highlights, and a few silver strands blended in as well.

I marveled at how amazing God was – giving me four different hair colors in one. Not one hair product on the market would be able to replicate it in the same manner.

I reached up and moved my hair, talking to God; praising Him for such complex things hidden in plain sight. Then I began to think about how God is called Abba, or Daddy.

"God, when I get to heaven, will I get to sit on Your lap and play with your beard like my kids used to play with my hair?"

I felt childish and a bit foolish for a moment. What kind of question was that to ask God? He's all-powerful. Why would I sit on His lap like a child? Still, I couldn't get the image out of my mind.

And then, God's presence enveloped me in a huge, comforting hug. Content, I headed into the church building and got my family situated.

During the pastor's sermon, my older son reached his long arm around my shoulders. And then he gently grabbed the end of my braid. His fingers started to play with it, just as he and his siblings had done as babies.

My breath caught in my throat. God, my Daddy, revealed Himself to me in that moment. My thoughts about our relationship were neither stupid nor childish. They were just right.

Thank you, Abba.

Eleven:
What's In a Name?

One year, as we typically did on Sunday afternoons, my family strolled through the local wholesale store in search of food samples and items we needed for the next few weeks. As we rounded a corner, I saw some old friends and stopped to chat. My boys noticed a tree in their cart and asked eagerly about it.

For over a decade, my children had wanted one for our yard. We just never seemed to find the right one, so our yard was one of the few on the block without shade or birds' nests. We found out the tree my friends were buying was a Chinese (Mormon) Apricot. To the surprise of our boys, my husband looked it up on his cell phone. What made them ecstatic was when he said it would be nice to get one.

In a moment's time, our casual shopping trip had a purpose. We stopped wandering the aisles and sought out the gardening area. Once there, we started playing a game of hide-and-seek among the rows of fruit trees, looking for the right kind and choosing the perfect one for our family.

At last, my husband placed the tree with its little box stand into the cart. Later, my mom would describe it as our "Charlie Brown" tree with one set of leaves sprouting on top and a little branch on the side.

The boys were proud of their tree and began discussing what to name it. A name was important to them because they'd learned how talking and singing to plants helped them grow better. So of course the tree couldn't remain nameless. One boy chose Moses, while the other asked me for options.

I said Moses was a good choice because the name could be a reminder of how the Israelite led God's People through the desert and how they were provided for during that time. I then suggested the names Joshua and Caleb might be nice as well. Joshua and Caleb were two spies who trusted God completely and wanted to take over the Promised Land right away, eventually getting to see it after 40 years in the wilderness.

The debate that had begun calmly escalated into a full argument, drawing the attention of the boys' father. After hearing the issue, he pointed out that Joshua couldn't work because there was an entire tree line with that name.

Trying to help the boys learn how to compromise, we then suggested that the tree could have two names. From that point on, our tree was dubbed Caleb Moses.

I think I'm beginning to understand how a person could care for a pet rock, or in our case, a pet tree. All my children cared for Caleb Moses, making sure it was watered and that the dirt around it was doing well. They even put earthworms in the area to help the soil. They greeted it in the morning on the way to school and again as they got home. They had a schedule in their minds of when the first harvest would come and how they would handle it. Caleb Moses had become precious in their eyes.

And though the Chinese (Mormon) Apricot tree was short in stature, time will tell if it will become like the children's story of "Clifford, the Big Red Dog" and grow enormous with love.

Twelve:
The Journey

I've heard many stories and accounts about what heaven will be like. As I've lost loved ones through the years, I have wondered more and more about the place. Will it all be gardens and light?

I know the Bible discusses the new heaven and earth when Jesus comes back, and I've pictured myself exploring them like crazy with Him by my side, teaching me new things.

I'll take time to just sit with Him and stare at the scenery for as long as we like and be in awe of His creativity. Will we be able to fly to get there? Like actually fly, without an airplane.

We'll sit and paint or sculpt; His being the creation itself, and me just trying to let Him see how I see it.

Of course there will be singing and praising around the clock. Choirs, quartets, maybe solos just for Him.

Most of all I picture all my dear family members meeting, greeting, playing, eating, and enjoying each other's company with Jesus in our midst.

Oh what a party and celebration that will be!

Thirteen:
D.O.G. Food

When I was a child, thinking about dog food didn't equate with hope. God used the year 2020 to change that for me and my family. I know most people automatically associate 2020 with the pandemic, but for my family, the trouble actually started about six months before that.

In the fall of 2019 my husband, who'd held a good job for almost two decades, was laid off. Because of his good work ethic, he received six weeks of severance pay from the vacation time he'd had stored up. With God's wisdom, we tightened our belts and managed to stretch the money to the beginning of December.

Meanwhile, my husband was proactive on looking for work and found a temporary job with a nonprofit, processing collected donations for the Christmas season. His new job started at the end of November and lasted through December.

God showed His creativity of providing for us again through the tax refunds in January. Again, we stretched all of it out as long as possible, amid rumors of a virus that was sweeping the country.

Then, the Pandemic hit and shut down the way society operated on a daily basis. I admit, I began to get concerned as the pantry and the dog food bin started running low.

But God. Remember I mentioned He's pretty creative? Some local churches and nonprofits started up bartering pages on social media to help people find resources. I may not have had money, but

I found I had things others wanted, and they also had what I needed.

During one particular memorable moment of concern, I had just scooped out a meal for my dogs and noticed I might have a day or two left before they ran out of food.

"Lord,', I prayed, "I know You'll provide for us, but I honestly can't see how You'll do it this time. My pantry is low, bills are coming up this week, and the dogs need more food now, too. Thank You for understanding. I'm trying not to stress, but God, please help my family. In Jesus Name, amen."

I continued with my daily tasks and then took a break to check one of the barter pages. A woman had posted that her dog was allergic to the brand of food she'd just bought, and it was free for the taking. I quickly messaged her. She called back, and we agreed to meet the next morning. I asked what I could give in return.

"Oh nothing, really," she graciously replied.

"Are you sure? We can figure something out." I wracked my brain for items a single lady might need or want. "I have some beef I could give you." I listed the different cuts I had left.

The woman's voice perked up on the other end. "I haven't had a roast in a while! That would be so nice!'

"It's a deal!" We both hung up happy with the way everything worked out.

I don't remember how God covered the finances that week, but He did. The next few months had a similar pattern: When the bills were due and the pantry was getting low, the dog food would also be running out. Each time, God would provide the dog food first, and then cover the bills and fill the pantry.

Yes, it took me a few months to figure it out, but His message to me was: I'm taking care of your dogs. How much more precious are you to Me, dear child? I've got your back. You can depend on Me.

In Matthew 6:25-26 Jesus says, "Therefore I tell you, do not be anxious about your life, what you will eat or what you will drink, nor about your body, what you will put on. Is not life more than food, and the body more than clothing? Look at the birds of the air: they neither sow nor reap nor gather into barns, and yet your heavenly Father feeds them. Are you not of more value than they?'

Now that I think about it, the acronym for D.O.G. is Depend On God. He was showing me that every time He gave me D.O.G. food, He was the answer to my problems all along.

Fourteen:
Cooking with Jesus

○ An Excerpt from my blog, *Pages for Life* ○

I had a dream that Jesus and I were making food in the kitchen, and we got to talking about spending time with Him in the Bible and just in general.

The more I listened and paid attention, the more He told me things. I asked what it was like for Him on the days I only read a scripture and then continued onto my day vs. when I took time to ponder His teachings.

He asked me what was for breakfast; I said eggs and some other things. He then proceeded to gather the ingredients and start making the eggs. Sometimes he asked others in the house for opinions on if they should be scrambled, boiled, etc. or where to find a pan and spatula, but pretty much ignoring me.

When the eggs were done, He sat down and looked at me. I understood that was the answer to my question.

When I don't take time to include Him, He's still there by my side, waiting to be acknowledged, ready to help and instruct. Instead I'm ignoring Him and seeking outside sources for the answers He has, or just doing things my own way. I let myself get distracted from what He has planned for me, or I flounder and wonder if it's going to work out. I miss out on a lot of rich, quality moments with Him, as well as those I'm meant to interact with and be part of the Body of Christ with.

All He wants is to be included in my life and have me seek Him first in everything, in the big moments and the small moments. He wants to have the kind of relationship where I naturally talk with Him about what's going on in life because He has the answers, and He knows the plans He has for me.

Fifteen:
Tomayto, Tomahto, Part Two

We'd just seen a miracle. The two boxes of tomatoes my husband and I carried into my mom's house were proof we didn't imagine it.

"What's all this?" mom asked over the loud jumble of my kids' chit chat.

The oldest one managed to be heard first, even through her excited giggles. "Nonna! God gave us tomatoes!"

Mom laughed. "Well I can see that! But where did they come from?"

All the kids talked over each other, but eventually she got the whole story.

"That's awesome! Let's put the green ones out on the table so they can ripen more easily." We all trooped into the dining room and set to work.

A few minutes later as I was relaxing, still warming up from the cold weather outside, I decided to check an online neighborhood group. Someone mentioned they had tomato plants in their driveway. Anyone could come take what they wanted. My husband and I decided to go look, since we liked to make sauces and could always use extra.

Mom watched the kids and we drove a few blocks away. Another person was already there, so we waited patiently as he perused the plants. A short time passed, and he went to leave, giving us a look that said "Good luck!"

Not to be dissuaded, we grabbed the medium sized gift bag my mom had handed us on the way out the door and crossed the street. We both found some green tomatoes here and there on the branches and placed them in the bag. As we double checked each branch, we found more.

And more.

And more again.

Enough to fill the entire bag to the brim, and still there were tomatoes on the branches. We looked at each other and laughed.

Back in the car, I realized one of my friends, who only lived a short distance away, might want some tomatoes, too.

"Let's swing by and see if she's home." I suggested.

J.E. answered the door. We heard music coming from the living room, where her family sat watching a TV show.

"Hey! It's great to see you! What's up?" she greeted us.

"Well, we have extra tomatoes, and we thought you might like some. They're still green, though."

"Oh, that won't be a problem! I can fry some up like that or let them ripen in a paper bag. Do you want to come in for a minute and warm up?" My blind friend turned and touched her cabinet as she went to orient herself to the room.

"Sure! Mom is watching the kids, so we have a few extra minutes." We followed her into her office/dining room area, where she turned to take the whole bag.

Now I admit, I had a brief moment of selfishness. Yes, we

had just seen God multiply tomatoes for us, twice. But for some reason, I wanted to still keep a few of these as well. It wasn't one of my finest moments, for sure, as I let her know my thoughts. "Oh, I was hoping to take a few home, too."

The instant look of disappointment in my best friend's face was enough to cut me to the quick, and I immediately repented to God for it, but I was too late for her response:

"That's all right. I'll grab a bowl, and you can pour in what you want to share." She handed the bag back.

Ouch.

I prayed again. *"Lord, I'm so sorry! I'll give it all to her willingly and cheerfully. Please forgive me, and please bless her abundantly."*

J.E. brought out a large, popcorn-sized bowl, and I poured the tomatoes in, to beyond overflowing. As I looked into the bag, I couldn't help but grin.

"J.E."

"Yes?"

"Feel the bag." My friend stuck her fingers into the opening and could tell the bag was three-fourths full still. "Oh, okay. Thank you."

"J.E., remember what we told you happened tonight at our place?"

"Yes…"

"Touch the bowl."

She reached out. "Oh my God!" Laughter escaped from all of us. "But the bag isn't empty!"

34

"I know! God just multiplied the tomatoes! Again! Grab another bowl!"

She got one that was half the size and again we filled it to overflowing.

The bag was only half empty. J.E. shared with us how God had multiplied food for her family and friends a few times, and we enjoyed each other's company, giving God all the glory and praise for what He had done, just because He could.

Sixteen:
Sun Tea

◦ An Excerpt from my blog, *Pages for Life* ◦

A few months ago, I bought a gallon sized jar of pickles. While I enjoy a dill or bread-and-butter pickle with my hamburger once in a while, this purchase was for a different end in my mind.

After my family finally ate the last of the pickles, I washed and rinsed the glass jar and lid and set it aside. We still had inclement weather, so I needed to wait for the next step.

At last we had a forecast of a hot and sunny day! I pulled out the large container I'd been storing for this purpose. I rummaged through my varieties of tea and found a favorite: mint. Placing a few tea bags in the jar, I filled it up with cold water and sealed it shut with the lid.

My Golden Retriever watched as I carefully brought the jar through the back door, down the steps, and started looking around. He followed with a toy in eager hopes we were about to play a game of fetch. I decided upon the perfect spot and set the jar on the cement sidewalk. My dog sniffed it and looked at me with questioning eyes.

"Not yet." I patted his head and walked over to another area where we could play with his tennis ball.

Throughout the day, I would glance out my kitchen window

and smile. Baking in the balmy weather, the water in the jar was turning an amber color. Thoughts of my mom drifted by on the breeze that fluttered the curtains. Echoes of children laughing and playing, adults talking, the scent of a barbeque grill cooking hot dogs and hamburgers, and bees hovering all came and went.

Finally, as my children set the table for dinner, I went back out and grabbed the jar. I carefully poured the tea into the waiting cups. Well, I started to, but I'd forgotten to take out the tea bags, and the first cup dumped all over the table. Whoops!

After cleaning up the spill and removing the tea bags, I actually did fill the cups for those who wanted some. Taking a refreshing sip, I sat back and watched how another generation started to make memories around a jar of sun tea.

1 Corinthians 3:10

"According to the grace of God given to me, like a skilled master builder I laid a foundation, and someone else is building upon it. Let each one take care how he builds upon it."

Seventeen:
Waffles and Ice Cream

Have you ever asked yourself how a family tradition started? From as far back as I can remember, one of my absolutely favorite dinners was waffles and ice cream. It was the perfect combination of a hot breakfast and a cold, cheap, boxed ice cream.

My mom would let us kids help her mix up the batter in a large bowl while she heated up the waffle iron. Then she would carefully spoon the batter onto the hot grids, close the lid, and lock it down. To this day I still wonder how she kept track of the timing with us kids distracting her, but she would know the exact moment when to reveal the golden deliciousness inside. Deftly she'd use a fork and pull the waffles onto each waiting plate. Quickly she'd use a large kitchen knife to slice a thick slab of ice cream from the rectangular treat and slap it onto one of them and covering it with the other waffle. The plate was then delivered to anxious hands and growling stomachs. I personally think she had to make a triple batch to keep up with us those nights.

It wasn't until years later when I was talking with my grandma that I discovered how this amazing dish became a family favorite. We'd been reminiscing about how she'd raised her kids through some tough economic times.

"T.D., there was this one time when I had no money and no groceries," she commented. "I looked through the cabinets and only found a little bit of something to make a few waffles, and I had a smidge of ice cream. I thought to myself, 'What am I going to do to feed these kids? Waffles are for breakfast, and ice cream isn't a meal, it's a dessert!'" Grandma looked directly at me. "I then took it to the Lord, because He is the one who provides, and He was going to be the one who provided then."

She gave a little laugh. "And wouldn't you know, He said, what's wrong with waffles and ice cream for dinner? So I thought, why not? And my kids LOVED it! They would ask me when we would have it again, and it became a family tradition to have every once in a while."

It makes me wonder what will become family traditions in my own children's lives because of a need that became a blessing.

Eighteen:
Tomayto, Tomahto, Part Three

In the Old Testament, Joshua is known for leading the Israelites into the Promised Land and defeating the city of Jericho. Something I also find fascinating is when they crossed the Jordan River on dry land before they entered.

The priests had to step into the rushing waters while it was in the flood season. God kept the river stopped up to allow the nation to cross, and the priests were instructed to hold the Arc of the Covenant in the middle of the river on dry ground. Once the nation crossed the river, the leaders were instructed to take 12 stones from the middle of the Jordan to set up on the far bank as memorial stones for future generations. Joshua placed 12 other stones back in the riverbed where the priests had stood as another set of memorial stones.

These days, setting up memorial stones isn't practiced in our society, but I have seen God placing memorial stones in the hearts and minds of people throughout their lives.

One of my biggest memorial stones happened the year He multiplied the tomatoes, just before the Pandemic.

My husband and I had just walked back into my mom's house carrying the paper gift bag half-full of green tomatoes. We couldn't wait to share with her and the kids the second miracle we'd witnessed that evening.

As we relayed what happened, all of us found spaces for

the tomatoes between the first batch on her dining room table. We also had to put some on a desk near the front living room window, the coffee table, the two end tables, and even some shelves. As my mom put it, "on every flat surface we could find room."

Through the weeks the initial excitement wore off, though the memory was still firmly etched into our minds. Every Sunday after church, my family would go to have lunch at my mom's place. Without fail, we'd inspect the tomato tables to see how they fared. After about a month, I began to grow concerned. Usually by now, at least some of the tomatoes would've turned red, yellow, or orange. However, they all stayed a consistent, pale green.

I decided to ask my mom about it. "How long does it take for a tomato to ripen off the vine?"

She thought a moment between making sandwiches. "Oh, maybe two or three days, maybe up to a week typically."

I frowned at our green tomatoes – which were now, according to theory, three weeks late. "Then why haven't these been turning different colors? Do you think we picked them too late?"

She looked at me, slightly confused. "What do you mean?"

"All of them are still green! Maybe something's wrong with them!"

Mom laughed. "No, I've been grabbing a generous handful every morning to pack in my lunch. That's usually what's been ripened by then."

My mind went back to that stormy evening when God had multiplied our tomatoes twice in one day. And then I laughed.

"Do you mean to say that you've been eating tomatoes, *from these very tables*, consistently for a month, and they're still *completely full*?"

Mom paused again, then smiled. "I never really thought about the fact they kept multiplying. I kept getting annoyed I couldn't consolidate them down to one table." We grinned at each other, thinking the same thing: God is so awesome!

I ran to get the others, excited to tell them how, yet again, God had chosen to bless us with multiplied tomatoes. The tables remained laden throughout the fall, winter, and into early spring – just before growing season – even with us eating them daily. As they ripened, we enjoyed the full smell of fresh tomatoes in the air and a rainbow of colorful beauty in the rooms. None of them ever spoiled or shriveled but were always just right each time.

God had truly created some very tasty memorial stones which would forever remind us in our hearts of His power, provision, and goodness.

What memorial stone has God given you to share with future generations?

Nineteen:
Pearls Under the Lamp Stand

Through the years as I grew up, I have distinct memories of sitting in a corner or at the dining room table listening to my adult family members shoot the breeze. They'd talk about their childhood and memories in the more recent past. Sometimes politics and religion would come up. I learned all sorts of things from most spectrums of thought for both sides. Our family was large enough to represent the polar opposites and everything in between.

What I appreciate about these times the most is that I also learned many lessons in wisdom. As they'd tout a tale, I'd learn what not to do as my relatives were pretty fearless, or how to handle tough situations. Sometimes I'd even learn a tip on how to cook well so as not to make the meal nasty.

Through it all, my grandmother would have her steady faith and unwavering smile as she enjoyed the company of her kids and grandkids. She never tired of me asking her questions about anything, and she always had a Scripture reference to relate to the topic at hand.

When my husband and I moved across the country a few years ago at the end of the Pandemic, both my grandma and I shed many tears. We gave each other enormous hugs, knowing it would be a while, and maybe not at all, for us to see each other this side of heaven. Thankfully my grandma had learned how to use her smart phone. We texted, chatted on the phone, and even had video calls quite often. Each time was like collecting another precious pearl of wisdom that I cherished and did my best to keep close.

Recently the opportunity came for me to go back and visit her and other members of my family. As we conversed, she agreed to have me "tape" record our discussions about her lifetime and anything that was important to her.

She repeated often, and always with a laugh, "I'm still learning, and when I get to heaven, I'll be taking 'Jesus 101'!" A beautiful image popped into my mind of my grandmother sitting at the feet of our Lord and Savior as Mary did when He walked the earth.

This, combined with the moments I was grateful to have with her, reminded me of a parable of Jesus. In it, a man finds a pearl of great price and sells everything he owns to buy it. Jesus was teaching us about His gift of salvation to any who would follow Him. I also remembered that Jesus is the Light and that He walks among the seven lamp stands.

I thought back on all my times with my grandma and how she shared her pearls with me through the reflective glow of Jesus' light in her life, and I realized:

I know what it looks like to find the Pearls under the Lampstand.

About
the
Author

T.D. Page is a full-time wife, mother, pet wrangler, and entrepreneur. She started creating stories when she was a little girl, and, because of the support of her friends, began putting them down on paper in middle school.

T.D.'s years as an Early Childhood Educator, a Special Needs mom, and a homeschool teacher, caused the books in her head to wait for the right moment to come out for the world to enjoy.

She hopes her readers will be inspired by the hope of Christ.

Works by
T.D. Page:

T.D.'s debut book, "**Mom's My Teacher?!**" helps moms and young students to see what homeschooling is all about in a kid-friendly picture book.

Her most recent publication, "**Pearls Under the Lampstand**", is an Inspirational book that documents how God has walked with her through different events in her life. It's written in the hope that the readers will see where God has also walked in their lives and draw encouragement from His presence.

T.D. Page is currently working on a Christian Dystopian novel called "**Fishers**" and hopes to finish it by the end of the year.

You can reach T.D. Page at writetdproductions@gmail.com and in her Facebook® group "Pearl Buddies".

Made in the USA
Columbia, SC
16 June 2025